SUCCESS BY THE WORD

Apostle
FRANCIS E. ANSO

Except otherwise stated, all scripture quotations are from the Authorized King James Version of the Holy Bible.

PRINTED & PUBLISHED BY

fireWord PUBLISHING

+2348039566773 | maikhetto@gmail.com

ISBN: 9798848473056

Cover & Interior Design: Maikhael Etto

APPRECIATION

I thank the Almighty God for His goodness to me and my family; for His knowledge bestowed upon me to write this book.

I am grateful to my lovely wife, Pastor (Mrs.) Mercy Francis Effiong, for she is a gift to me from the Most High.

I will not forget to appreciate my lovely children: Emem, Asuquo, and Ekemini. I am especially grateful to God for my daughter, Uduak, for her efforts to help me succeed with my dreams and aspirations.

I want to also thank Evang. (Mrs.) Mary Anthony Okon and her brother, Pastor Maikhael Etto, for working with me in the production of this book from start to finish. Your efforts are highly appreciated.

I will not fail to appreciate all the members of Land of Truth Fellowship for their love, support, and encouragement.

I pray that the good Lord – the One who blesses all men, and the Rewarder of those who diligently seek Him - should bless and reward you all, in the name of Jesus. Amen.

TABLE OF CONTENTS

INTRODCUTION

I remember sometimes in 1982, when the Lord ministered to me through one Pastor Effiom that I will become a priest unto Him, whether I liked it or not.

After twelve years the Lord ministered the same message again through one Clan Head in Bakassi in 1993. After this second message, something terrible happened to me – I lost everything and returned home empty handed.

After this, I struggled to establish myself but to no avail. In 1997 I made up my mind to return to Bakassi to start life afresh, but I did not tell my wife. Soon after, the Lord ministered to me through my wife, asking me if I wanted to run away and return to Bakassi. The Lord asked me if I wanted what happened to Jonah to happen to me, and then warned me not to try it otherwise I would suffer severe consequences.

The Lord asked me to study the Book of Jonah and when I did, I wept like a child. At that, I decided to surrender totally to God and to His plan and purpose for my life. I joined the Mount Zion Light House Full Gospel Church and became a fully committed member of the church. I began to serve the Lord as an usher in the church.

Though it was not easy for me because of the hard times I was going through, I did my best to serve the Lord enthusiastically with all my heart and strength.

In 1998 the Lord ministered to me through one Prophetess Rebecca and the next year my wife became pregnant, and we were so happy for the Lord had visited us, just like He visited Hannah and Elkanah in the Bible.

It was that same year, 1999, that armed robbers broke into our house at night, and they beat me up and robbed us of our valuable belongings. I was left with nothing except the clothe I had on me. Our condition became worse.

It looked as though there was no hope for me and my family. I know before I gave my life to Christ, I used to indulge in smoking, drinking, except stealing. But when this terrible incident happened to me and my family, I broke down and wept. When I remembered how hard I had struggled before and then lost everything, I wondered why all of these would happen to me, though I was called to me a servant of God. This even made me weep the more.

But in spite of all these, we did not slack in our faith in God and in our duties as servants of God. I decided to abandon my fate into the hands of God Almighty who knows all things.

In the year 2000 my wife gave birth to a baby girl whom we named Uduak. From that year, things began to change for the better. God began to give us one open door after another and since then things have only become better. After all those years of hardship, the Lord prospered us and blessed us with the desires of our hearts.

Before I came to Christ, I used to be a very stubborn person who was feared by many. But God has transformed my personality to a humble and forgiving person.

I have been serving the Lord as a priest since 2002 until 2012 when I was ordained an Apostle in the Body of Christ. But the work of the Lord is not about titles; it's about doing the work of God and walking in His will.

Our religious titles do not qualify us to enter into the Kingdom of Heaven; doing the Word of God is the ultimate thing.

> *"And he saith unto me, Seal not the sayings of the prophecy of this book: for the time is at hand. And, behold, I come quickly; and my reward is with me, to give every man according as his work shall be. I am Alpha and Omega, the beginning and the end, the first and the last. Blessed are they that do his commandments, that they may have right to the tree of life, and may enter in through the gates into the city." Revelation 22:10, 12- 14*

The blessing comes from doing His Word. Eternal life comes from doing His Word. No matter what a man has achieved and accumulated in this life, if he cannot enter in through the gates into the city of God to access God's tree of life, then his time on earth was wasted.

We can never succeed in life, in our calling, or in doing whatever God created us to do, except by His Word. Knowing and doing the Word of God is the secret to success. Matthew 25:23 says,

> *"His lord said unto him, Well done, good and faithful servant; thou hast been faithful over a few things, I will make thee ruler over many things: enter thou into the joy of thy lord."*

Only the Word of God can make us become good and faithful servants of God. This is why I have written this book – to impress on us the eternal importance of God's Word to the short time of our sojourn on earth.

We all have our story, just as I have briefly shared mine with you. But no matter our story and our experiences in life, if we do not have an experience with the Word of God, then we have no story that is of interest to heaven; and we have no story to tell when we step into eternity.

Therefore, I encourage you to read with this and pay attention to it with all your heart, for in it are thoughts and insights that will enable you achieve all-round success.

God bless you.

Chapter 1

THE NECESSITY OF THE WORD

The Word of God is crucial to every aspect of our lives as believers. Without the Word of God we cannot know the will of God, we cannot live the life of God, and we cannot see the Kingdom of God. We cannot walk in obedience to God's Word if we do not have knowledge of His Word.

The reason many believers do not live according to the instruction of God's Word is because they do not fellowship with the Word of God; they do not study and meditate on the Word. They prefer to spend time with worthless people or doing worthless things than to spend time with the Word of God.
However, the Word of God influences our association and choice of companions. If we know the Word of God and allow it to influence and direct our lives, we cannot keep company with worthless people. For instance, 1Corinthians 5:9-11 says,

"In the letter that I wrote you I told you not to associate with immoral people. Now I did not mean pagans who are immoral or greedy or are thieves, or who worship idols. To avoid them you would have to get out of the world completely. What I meant was that you should not associate with a person who calls himself a believer but is immoral or greedy or worships idols or is a slanderer or a drunkard or a thief. Don't even sit down to eat with such a person." (GNB)

It is a pity that many people who call themselves Christians, who are workers in the church, and even hold leadership positions in church, still practice idol worship and pagan customs that have nothing to do with the Word of God and the life that Christ has called us to live. They are very active in church, yet their lifestyle is very far from the life of Christ. They profess to know Christ, yet they deny him in their works – their words, actions, and behavior.

The Word of God is important to our destinies because it determines where we will spend eternity. Unless we know the word of God we can never do the works of God. A believer who does not know the Word of God can never talk like a child of God or behave like a child of God. The Bible says,

"Do you not know that the unrighteous will not inherit the kingdom of God? Do not be deceived, neither fornicators, nor idolaters, nor adulterers, nor homosexuals, nor sodomites, nor thieves, nor covetous, nor drunkards, nor revilers, nor extortioners will inherit the kingdom of God."
1Corinthians 6:9-10, NKJV

This scripture show that people who profess to be Christians but do not practice the Word of God are merely deceiving themselves. People who are very religious but refuse to live by the instruction of God's Word are merely deceiving themselves. People cannot deceive God because God sees and knows every man's work and will recompense every man according to his works.

The Fear of the Lord Is A Product of God's Word

We are living in the last days and the world has changed rapidly. Back in the old days, you could easily differentiate between a believer and an unbeliever. But today, that is no longer the case. All manners of sins and atrocities are committed by people you ordinarily would not expect to do such things.

Nowadays, you can hardly take people by their word, even in the church. The level of falsehood, dishonesty and fraudulence in the church is alarming. It is now a common thing for people to stand in God's presence, on God's altar and tell lies without any fear of God; and these are people who profess to be children of God.

For instance, when people find themselves in one trouble or the other, they often come running to church to meet God's servant to pray for them. They make pledges and promises to God that if God should help them out of their problem or get what they desire, they will do one thing or the other for God and for the church.

However, after the servant of God has prayed for them and God visits them and help them out of their problems or to get that which they had desired, they fail to fulfill their promises to God. God has helped many people who came running to Him to get to several positions of power and authority, but after they got there they forget about God and the pledge they made before God and instead they begin to worship other gods for protection. The Bible says,

> *"So when you make a promise to God, keep it as quickly as possible. He has no use for a fool. Do what*

you promise to do. Better not to promise at all than to make a promise and not keep it. Don't let your own words lead you into sin, so that you have to tell God's priest that you didn't mean it. Why make God angry with you? Why let him destroy what you have worked for?" Ecclesiastes 5:4-6, GNB

If those other gods were that powerful, why didn't they seek the help of those gods when they were in trouble and when they were seeking breakthrough? How can you run to another god to help you protect and keep a breakthrough he could not give to you? How can a god who cannot give you life protect your life? How can an idol that was carved by the hands of men protect you from men?

Apart from seeking other gods to protect them, they multiply their iniquity by seeking to bring down the people whom God used to bless and establish them. For some ministers of God, their biggest enemies and antagonists are the very people God used them to bless and uplift. Because they do not want to fulfill their vows to God and to the church, they try to bring down the church and the ministers of God.

But they forget that the God who lifted them up can also bring them down (1Samuel 2:2-9); they forget that the anointing that took Saul to the throne was also ***the anointing that removed him from the throne. You cannot fight God's anointed whose anointing has blessed your life.*** You cannot bite the hand that feeds you and expect to keep on eating.

People who refuse to redeem their vow to God simply show that they are foolish because God cannot be mocked (Galatians 6:7). ***People who try to make a mockery of God end up making a mockery of themselves.*** Their fraudulence shows lack reverence for God, and their irreverence for God is due to the fact that they do not know the Word of God.

Doing The Word

"But be ye doers of the word, and not hearers only, deceiving your own selves." James 1:22

But how can people do the Word if they don't take to heart the word they hear to mediate and reflect on it? The Good News Bible says, *"Do not deceive yourselves by just listening to his word; instead, put it into practice."* To practice means to learn something by doing it repeatedly. It may be difficult, but as we keep on practicing it we become good at it and accustomed to it.

Moreover, how can people do the Word if they don't know the Word? Some people don't have a habit of studying the Word at home and they are also infrequent in church to hear the Word of God. People cannot do the Word until they know the Word.

When people keep themselves from knowing the Word they keep themselves from living righteously. Your ignorance of God's Word is not an excuse because such is willful ignorance. Unlike in ancient times, the Word of God is now available everywhere for people to access – in print, on the internet, and on mobile phones. There are free Bibles everywhere. The Word of God says,

> *"And the times of this ignorance God winked at; but now commandeth all men every where to repent"*
> *Acts 17:30*

The truth is that, ***you're either a doer of the Word or a doer of evil.***

People who indulge in murder, slander, armed robbery, rape, kidnapping, adultery, and sexual pervasions can be found in our churches today. People who commit ritual murder and perform human sacrifices for money, for government position and for business breakthrough, can be found in our churches, and some of them even occupy positions of leadership in our churches. After doing all of these, they expect their offerings and tithes to be acceptable to God.

Some ministers have twisted the gospel of prosperity by encouraging their congregation to get money by whatever means they can and then give part of the money to God, so that it will be sanctified. However, ***the fact that your pastor is not concerned about how you make your money does not mean that God is not.***

No matter how much you give to a church or to a man of God, if your money is a product of ill-gotten wealth and you do not practice the Word of God, God will eventually deny knowing you and say to you "Depart from Me, all you workers of iniquity" (Luke 13:27, NKJV).

The fact that your pastor has accepted that ill-gotten money does not mean that God has accepted it. All your ill-gotten money cannot buy you salvation. ***All the money in the world cannot get you a ticket to heaven. Prosperity is not a sin, but it is a sin to seek prosperity at all cost***. This is why it is important for people to know the Word of God so that they will not be deceived by some fake and fraudulent ministers who are only interested in personal gain.

Ungodly Church Leaders

The Bible already foretold and forewarned us about what people will be like in the end-time church. It says,

> *"But know this, that in the last days perilous times will come. For men will be lovers of themselves, lovers of money, boasters, proud, blasphemers, disobedient to parents, unthankful, unholy, unloving, unforgiving, slanders, without self-control, brutal, despisers of good, traitors, headstrong, haughty, lovers of pleasure rather than lovers of God, having a form of godliness but denying its power. And from such people turn away!" 2Timothy 3:1-5*

Some Bishops, Apostles, Pastors, Prophets, Prophetesses, Deacons, Deaconesses, and Choristers are very far from the Word of God. They may look pious from afar, but if you happen to get close to them you will be shocked that some of them do not really know the Lord or practice the Word of God.

They bear religious titles and claim to be messengers of God, but if you observe their behavior and lifestyle you will know that they are not really children of God. They tolerate all manners of ungodly behavior and ungodly dressing in their churches because they themselves are ungodly.

They do not care if their members dress half-naked to church or that their men, especially the married men, are using some of the single sisters in church. The main reason they overlook these things is because they are ungodly leaders who are far from the Word of God.

Many people occupying positions of leadership in our churches are idol worshipers who 'worship' God in the daytime before everyone, but at night they worship other gods in the presence of a selected few. The Word of God says,

> *"I do not want you to be partners with demons. You cannot drink the cup of the Lord and the cup of demons. You cannot take part in the table of the Lord and the table of demons." 1Corinthians 10:20-21, NIV*

Churchgoers vs. Children of God

There is a difference between churchgoers and children of God. Churchgoers are those who go to church for various reasons, but God's children are those who know God and worship Him in spirit and in truth.

Similarly, there is a difference between a church leader and a servant of God; ***you can be a church leader and not be a servant of God.*** A church leader is someone who occupies a position of leadership in the church, but a servant of God is one who has been called by God and lives by the Word of God, and who serves the Lord faithfully.

The difference between a serious believer and an unserious believer is the knowledge and practice of the Word of God. The difference between a genuine man of God and a fake man of God is the knowledge and practice of the Word of God.

We cannot know God if we do not know His Word; we cannot properly serve God if we do not know His Word. The Word of God makes the difference between spirituality and carnality. In 2Corintians 6:2 the Lord says,

> *'"In an acceptable time I have heard you, and in the day of salvation I have helped you." Behold, now is the accepted time; behold, now is the day of salvation.' (NKJV)*

Therefore, this is the time to change, to change from idol worship to true worship, to change from selfishness to selflessness; to change from godless living to righteous living, to change from religious hypocrisy to true Christianity; to change from falsehood and fraudulence to truthfulness; and this change will only happen when we decide to fall in love with the Word of God and live by it.

Mark 1:14-15 says Jesus came "preaching the gospel of the kingdom of God, and saying, the time is fulfilled, and the kingdom of God is at hand: repent ye, and believe the gospel."

People who think they still have a lot of time to play around are simply deceiving themselves. The safest insurance for eternity is to believe the gospel NOW and live by it.

Chapter 2
TIMELESS LESSONS FROM DANIEL

One of the reasons many people lack the fear of God is because they do not see God with their eyes. They make light of God's Word and instructions because God cannot be seen.

Daniel was human just like us; he never saw God with his eyes throughout his lifetime. Yet the Bible records that he was so faithful and diligent in living by God's instruction, such that there was no error or fault found in him. His enemies searched for something bad with which they could bring him down but found nothing.

Out of frustration, they now plotted to destroy him through his acts of righteousness and obedience to God's Law. The Bible says,

> *"Then this Daniel was preferred above the presidents and princes, because an excellent spirit was in him; and the king thought to set him over the whole realm. Then the presidents and princes sought to find occasion against Daniel concerning the*

kingdom; but they could find none occasion nor fault; forasmuch as he was faithful, neither was there any error or fault found in him. Then said these men, We shall not find any occasion against this Daniel, except we find it against him concerning the law of his God."
Daniel 6:3-5

Daniel lived in one of the most morally decadent and diabolic society in human history, yet he was not morally decadent and he did not engage in diabolic activities.

This shows that believers today who use the moral decadence in the society as an excuse for their unrighteous living are merely deceiving themselves. People live in sin, not because the world has become a very sinful place, but because they choose to do so.

You Have No Excuse

Have you ever wondered that ***no one was ever allowed to enter heaven because he had excuses for his sin***? God says,

"Therefore thou art inexcusable, O man, whosoever thou art ..." Romans 2:1

Daniel did not use the sinfulness and corruption in Babylon as an excuse to live in sin. He worked in the government of Babylon, yet he was not corrupted by the corruption in Babylon.

However, there are many people today who cannot serve God or walk uprightly just because they occupy one government position or the other. There are people who think it is impossible for one to be in government and serve God faithfully. However, Daniel proves them wrong.

Daniel occupied one of the highest political positions in Babylon, yet he remained faithful to God. The Bible says,

> *"Then the king made Daniel great and gave him many great gifts, and he made him to rule over the whole province of Babylon and to be chief governor over all the wise men of Babylon. And Daniel requested of the king and he appointed Shadrach, Meshach, and Abednego over the affairs of the province of Babylon. But Daniel remained in the gate of the king [at the king's court]." Daniel 2:48-49, AMP*

Nebuchadnezzar made him ruler over the whole province of Babylon, yet Daniel still found time to pray to God. But there are people who occupy lesser positions in government yet they no longer have time for God. There are people who think they have arrived and that they no longer need God, just because of the little position they have come to occupy in government.

Daniel proves that no matter your position in government, you have no excuse not to serve God and walk in his ways. No matter how high the position you occupy in government, ***you can never be too big to serve God***. In spite of his high position in Babylon, second only to Nebuchadnezzar, Daniel humbled himself before God to live according to God's ways. The Bible says,

> *"When Daniel learned that the order had been signed, he went home. In an upstairs room of his house there were windows that faced toward Jerusalem. There, just as he had always done, he knelt down at the open windows and prayed to God three times a day."*
> *Daniel 6:10, GNB*

This shows that Daniel practiced prayer as a daily routine. It was part of his lifestyle and not something he did once in a while or when he was in trouble. In spite of his position of power and affluence, Daniel had a habit of seeking God's face and spending time in God's presence.

The devil orchestrated this event to stop Daniel from praying and to separate him from his God. But Daniel was not ignorant of the devices of the devil and refused to be intimidated into abandoning his faith.

Many people who occupy high positions in government and in the corporate world have been intimidated into abandoning God because of their ignorance. They seek protection for their lives and positions by joining secret societies to fraternize with demons and satanic deities. What they don't know is that doing so will not protect but destroy their lives and their families.

Seeking protection from the devil is like hiring armed robbers and terrorists to protect your most valuable treasures. The Bible says the devil came to steal, kill, and destroy; he did not come to bless, protect, and establish you (John 10:10). Therefore, ***it is foolish to seek help and security from the enemy of your destiny***. The Bible says,

> *"Therefore be glad (exult), O heavens and you that dwell in them! But woe to you, O earth and sea, for the devil has come down to you in fierce anger (fury),*

because he knows that he has [only] a short time [left]!" Revelation 12:12, AMP

The devil did not come down to earth with a loving heart to help you and protect you. He came down with resentment and violent intent, which is why the devil is not your friend. ***If you seek help from the devil, you're merely helping the devil to destroy you.***

You Cannot Be Too Big To Live By the Word

The scripture quote above says Daniel would pray in *"an upstairs room of his house"*. This shows that Daniel lived in a duplex. Daniel lived about 500 years before the time of Christ, that is about 2, 500 years ago, yet he lived in a luxurious upstairs apartment; something that many people today use as a source of pride and arrogance. No wonder the Bible says there is nothing new under the sun (Ecclesiastes 1:9).

No matter what you possess, you have no justification to be proud before God because there is nothing you have that was not given to you (1Corinthians 4:7); there is nothing you have that another person did not already have.

No matter the kind of house you live in, people have lived in that kind of house and yet they still humble themselves to serve and worship God. No matter the kind of car you drive, people have driven that kind of car and yet they still worship God and live godly lives.

If you think you have become too big to serve God and that people should come and bow to you because of your expensive cars, what about the person who designed and built that expensive car you bought? No matter how big you think your expensive car has made you, you cannot be bigger than the person who designed and built that car.

The people who designed and built that car deserve more honors and respect than you the consumer. Isn't it funny that some of the people who designed the car you are driving are humbly serving God, yet you have become too proud to serve God because of the same car?

All these goes to show that ***there is nothing in this world that is worth taking the place of God in our lives.*** What you have is nothing compared to what God has in store for you. When you despise God because of those things, you miss out on the bigger things God has in store for you.

Faithfulness Guarantees Victory

When those highly placed politicians in Babylon, who were intimidated by Daniel's competence and jealous of his position, came up with a plan that would require Daniel to compromise his faith and go against the commandments of his God, they thought they were going to succeed against Daniel. The Bible says,

> *Then these presidents and satraps came [tumultuously] together to the king and said to him, King Darius, live forever! All the presidents of the kingdom, the deputies and the satraps, the counselors and the governors, have consulted and agreed that the king should establish a royal statute and make a firm decree that whoever shall ask a petition of any god or man for thirty days, except of you, O king, shall be cast into the den of lions.*
>
> *Now, O king, establish the decree and sign the writing that it may not be changed, according to the law of the Medes and Persians, which cannot be altered. So King Darius signed the writing and the decree."*
>
> *Daniel 6: 6-9, AMP*

Yet Daniel refused to compromise. He knew he would lose his position, his wealth, and his life by going against the unrighteous decree the king had signed into law. However, Daniel preferred to lose these things than to lose his God. He valued his relationship and right standing with God more than his relationship and good standing with the king. He preferred to be separated from the king than to be separated from his God.

> *"Then the king commanded, and Daniel was brought and cast into the den of lions. The king said to Daniel, May your God, Whom you are serving continually, deliver you! And a stone was brought and laid upon the mouth of the den, and the king sealed it with his own signet and with the signet of his lords, that there might be no change of purpose concerning Daniel. Then the king went to his palace and passed the night fasting, neither were instruments of music or dancing girls brought before him; and his sleep fled from him." Daniel 6:16-18, AMP*

When the king threw Daniel into the lions' den, his enemies who plotted against him were happy with themselves because they thought they had finally destroyed Daniel. But to their greatest shock, the lions refused to eat Daniel because the God he served faithfully had sent His angels to shut the mouths of the lions. Instead of the lions to attack him they became friendly with him, just like it was with Adam in the Garden of Eden.

"Then the king arose very early in the morning and went in haste to the den of lions. And when he came to the den and to Daniel, he cried out in a voice of anguish. The king said to Daniel, O Daniel, servant of the living God, is your God, Whom you serve continually, able to deliver you from the lions?
Then Daniel said to the king, O king, live forever!
My God has sent His angel and has shut the lions' mouths so that they have not hurt me, because I was found innocent and blameless before Him; and also before you, O king, [as you very well know] I have done no harm or wrong." Daniel 6:19-22, AMP

This shows that God is always faithful to those who remain faithful to him. ***If you risk everything to serve and follow God, God will go any extent to protect, bless, and lift you up.*** Your commitment to God is not a waste, for when you are in need of Him, He will show up and intervene on your behalf. Deuteronomy 7:9 says,

"Know therefore that the LORD thy God, he is God, the faithful God, which keepeth covenant and mercy with them that love him and keep his commandments to a thousand generations."

The scripture says when Daniel was thrown into the lions' den the king placed a seal on the entrance to the den *"that there might be no change of purpose concerning Daniel."* It does not matter what people have done and sealed concerning your life and destiny, it does not matter what people have concluded concerning you, if you live by God's Word and serve Him faithfully, He will upturn and overturn every evil purpose that was sealed against your destiny. No matter what they said cannot be changed regarding your destiny God will change things in your favor and cause all things to work out for your good.

When you serve God faithfully, the things that destroy others will not destroy you. Psalm 31:23 says, "Love the LORD, all his faithful people. The LORD protects the faithful, but punishes the proud as they deserve" (GNB). If you want your life, your family, and all you have worked for to be preserved, serve the Lord faithfully. Your preservation is in your faithfulness to God and not in running after false gods.

It's also interesting to note that as God delivered Daniel from the desires of his enemies, He also rewarded them according to their works. The same lions that refused to eat Daniel feasted on his enemies immediately they were thrown into the lions' den. This shows that ***all you need to do to bring your enemies to shame and defeat is by remaining faithful to the Lord.*** Your faithfulness to

God will provoke Him to rise up against the wicked who seek to destroy you.

Understanding Is Crucial

What was the secret to Daniel staying faithful to God? It's because he did not let the Word of God to be far from him. He loved the Lord because he loved the Word of God. He said,

"I Daniel understood by books…" Daniel 9:2

The understanding necessary to live a successful life can only be acquired from The Book – the Word of God.

There are things we can never understand about God, about life, and about ourselves, if we do not know the Word of God. It takes understanding to live a godly life, and that understanding comes from the Word of God.

The reason Daniel did not compromise his faith is because of some understanding he acquired from the Book. The reason he developed a habit of prayer and continued in it, even under the threat of death, is because of some understanding he acquired from the Book. The reason Daniel was so competent and successful as a government official is because of some understanding he acquired from the Book.

One of the reasons people live below God's standard, fail in life, or feel too proud to serve God, is because they are yet to acquire some understanding from the Book.

Chapter 3

LEARNING FROM MORDECAI & ESTHER

Mordecai and Esther were people whose lives and beliefs were shaped by knowledge of God's Word. They played vital roles in the frustration of Haman who sought to annihilate the Jews.

Right from the outset even when Haman's motive and intentions were not yet known, Mordecai could discern that Haman was not a friend of the Jewish people, but an enemy of God. Because of this, Mordecai refused to cow down before Haman to massage his ego. He refused to be intimidated by Haman's personality or position of power. He showed courage and refused to be a coward.

> *"Haman went away that day joyful and elated in heart. But when he saw Mordecai at the king's gate refusing to stand up or show fear before him, he was*

filled with wrath against Mordecai. Nevertheless, Haman restrained himself and went home."
Esther 5:9-10, AMP

Haman hated Mordecai because of this and especially because Mordecai was a Jew. He became proud and boastful about his wealth and position of power; and began to plan a special death for Mordecai.

"And Haman recounted to them the glory of his riches, the abundance of his [ten] sons, all the things in which the king had promoted him, and how he had advanced him above the princes and servants of the king. Haman added, Yes, and today Queen Esther did not let any man come with the king to the dinner she had prepared but myself; and tomorrow also I am invited by her together with the king.
Yet all this benefits me nothing as long as I see Mordecai the Jew sitting at the king's gate. Then Zeresh his wife and all his friends said to him, Let a gallows be made, fifty cubits [seventy-five feet] high, and in the morning speak to the king, that Mordecai may be hanged on it; then you go in merrily with the king to the dinner. And the thing pleased Haman, and he caused the gallows to be made."
Esther 5:11-14, AMP

However, it takes a man who has deep faith in God and in His Word to do what Mordecai did. He was confident that the Word of God will not fail. Even in the face of the threat that such a powerful man as Haman posed to him, he was not afraid for his life. He knew that the Word of God abides forever and that Haman was just a temporary threat that God could deal with.

It takes the devil to produce people like Haman and it takes the Word of God to produce people like Mordecai and Esther. If Mordecai and Esther were not mindful of God's Word, they would have worked to save just themselves. But because they knew God's plan and purpose for His people, they worked to save the entire Jewish population from destruction.

It's interesting to know that while Haman was plotting to kill Mordecai, God was planning to honor Mordecai and humiliate Haman in the process. God humiliated him when he was ordered by the king to dress up Mordecai in royal robes and parade him through the city square on the king's horse.

> *"Then the king said to Haman, Make haste and take the apparel and the horse, as you have said, and do so to Mordecai the Jew, who sits at the king's gate. Leave out nothing that you have spoken.*

Then Haman took the apparel and the horse and conducted Mordecai on horseback through the open square of the city, proclaiming before him, Thus shall it be done to the man whom the king delights to honor. Then Mordecai came again to the king's gate. But Haman hastened to his house, mourning and having his head covered." Esther 6:10-12, AMP

After this humiliation, his wife, friends, and advisers warned him that it was dangerous for him to keep planning to kill Mordecai because Mordecai was a child of God. Therefore, Mordecai's enemies knew he was an uncompromising child of God, and they feared him because of this.

How can we claim to be children of God and the workers of darkness do not fear us? How can we claim to be servants of God and those who serve the devil do not see a difference in us? Only the Word of God can make a difference in our lives. Only the Word of God can make us different. People who do not give themselves to the Word of God can hardly be different from the worldly people around them.

Living by the Word of God is what will make us to stand out and shine in a dark, wicked, and corrupt world. You can never be like Mordecai and Esther except you have the Word of God in you. You can never stand up to the Hamans in your generation except you are standing on the Word of God; for only those who stand on the Word of God can stand up for God.

People who are not sure of their stand can never be used by God to accomplish great things. God used Mordecai and Esther to accomplish great things in their generation because they stood firm on God's Word and Covenant.

> *"Then Mordecai told them to return this answer to Esther, Do not flatter yourself that you shall escape in the king's palace any more than all the other Jews. For if you keep silent at this time, relief and deliverance shall arise for the Jews from elsewhere, but you and your father's house will perish. And who knows but that you have come to the kingdom for such a time as this and for this very occasion?"*
> *Esther 4:13-14, AMP*

In spite of her position as queen, surrounded by wealth and opulence, Esther still humbled herself to listen to Mordecai's rebuke and instruction. But if some of us were to occupy similar position we would no longer listen to our pastors when they rebuke or instruct us; we would think that our high position in government has placed us above our pastors and spiritual leaders.

God knew the hearts of Esther and Mordecai; He knew that their hearts were transformed by His Word, which is why He lifted them up to such high positions. Esther was an orphan girl in a foreign land, yet God raised her up to be queen over the native-born women of the land. Mordecai used to sit at the gate of the palace, yet God raised him up to occupy a high position of influence in the king's court.

"And all the princes of the provinces and the chief rulers and the governors and they who attended to the king's business helped the Jews, because the fear of Mordecai had fallen upon them. For Mordecai was great in the king's palace; and his fame went forth throughout all the provinces, for the man Mordecai became more and more powerful." Esther 9:3-4, AMP

However, God did not end there; He further elevated him to become the Prime Minister of Persia.

"Mordecai the Jew was second in rank only to King Xerxes himself. He was honored and well-liked by his fellow Jews. He worked for the good of his people and for the security of all their descendants."
Esther 10:3, GNB

While they were nothing, Mordecai and Esther remained faithful to the Lord, continuing in His ways. They did not abandon the Word of God to seek their own way of making it in life; they did not manipulate their way to those high positions, but God lifted them up and made them outstandingly successful because of their commitment to the Word of His Covenant. James 4:10 says,

> *"Humble yourselves [feeling very insignificant] in the presence of the Lord, and He will exalt you [He will lift you up and make your lives significant]." AMP*

Humility before God leads to elevation before men. ***You cannot kneel down before God and not be able to stand up before men.*** You cannot make yourself insignificant before God and not become significant before men. ***When you succeed in doing the Word of God, you have no choice but to become successful in life.***

In spite of her position as queen, surrounded by the best of every good thing in life, Esther humbled herself to wait on the Lord in fasting and prayer for her people.

> *"Then Esther told them to give this answer to Mordecai, Go, gather together all the Jews that are present in Shushan, and fast for me; and neither eat nor drink*

> *for three days, night or day. I also and my maids will fast as you do. Then I will go to the king, though it is against the law; and if I perish, I perish."*
> *Esther 4:15-16, AMP*

This shows that she was someone who had been practicing fasting and prayer before that time. She was not just a hearer of the Word, but a doer also. She was not motivated to fast by her personal problems, but because of her people. How many of our leaders would fast and pray for the welfare of their people?

We often preach that the people should fast and pray for their leaders, but here we see Esther fasting and praying for her people. All was well with her, yet she fasted and prayed because all was not well with her people. This is a sterling example of godly leadership.

We also see in this scripture that Esther risked her life for her people, which shows that she was not selfish and self-centered. She did not love and value her position more than the life of her people. There are things people cannot do except they have the Word of God in them. Only the Word of God can produce the outstanding qualities and sterling character that are expected of leaders. ***People whose***

lives are not influenced by God's Word cannot lead by God's influence.

It is never the perfect will of God that His people should be led by those who do not have His Word in their hearts, because the Word of God is the will of God. If you do not know the Word of God, then you do not know the will of God for your life, for the position you occupy, and for the people you lead or seek to lead. Because of his knowledge of God's will (Word), Mordecai understood that God had positioned Esther as queen to save the Jewish people from extermination.

Until you know the Word of God you cannot understand why God has made you who you are, why you are where you are, why you are working where you are, why you are with the person you're with, why you are serving where you are, and why God elevated you to your present position.

Without knowledge of the Word, opportunities are wasted and destinies frustrated.

Chapter 4

LESSONS FROM THREE REMARKABLE YOUNG MEN

Shadrach, Meshach, and Abednego were three young men who proved that people who do not live by the Word of God cannot have the courage to stand in defense of the Word. A wise man once said that until you have something to live for, you have nothing to die for.

By their readiness to die for their faith in the Lord and for the truth of His Word, Shadrach, Meshach, and Abednego showed that they lived by the Word of God and had unshakeable faith in the Word.

These three young men were among the captives who were taken from Jerusalem and exiled to Babylon by King Nebuchadnezzar. Upon arrival in Babylon they were expected to live by the laws and instructions of their slave masters. They were expected to live according to the ways of the Babylonians and worship the gods of Babylon.

But these three young men refused to abandon their God no matter what. They refused to let the fear of man deviate them from the ways of their God. The Bible says,

> *"Nebuchadnezzar the king [caused to be] made an image of gold, whose height was sixty cubits or ninety feet and its breadth six cubits or nine feet. He set it up on the plain of Dura in the province of Babylon. Then Nebuchadnezzar the king sent to gather together the satraps, the deputies, the governors, the judges and chief stargazers, the treasurers, the counselors, the sheriffs and lawyers, and all the chief officials of the provinces to come to the dedication of the image which King Nebuchadnezzar had [caused to be] set up.*
> *Then the satraps, the deputies, the governors, the judges and chief stargazers, the treasurers, the counselors, the sheriffs and lawyers, and all the chief officials of the provinces were gathered together for the dedication of the image that King Nebuchadnezzar had set up, and they stood before the image that Nebuchadnezzar had set up." Daniel 3:1-3, AMP*

Nebuchadnezzar commanded that at the sound of the horn, flute, harp, and other musical instruments, everyone must bow to the ground and worship his gold statue – everyone despite their office and position, and whatever their race, tribe, nation, or language.

Nebuchadnezzar also decreed that anyone who disobeyed this command would be immediately thrown into a burning fiery furnace.

King Nebuchadnezzar was worshipped like a god in Babylon; his words were law, and nobody ever dared to disobey his command. But for the first time in his life, Nebuchadnezzar was shocked when it was reported to him that some people had refused to obey his command to serve his gods and bow down in worship of his gold statue.

> *"Therefore at that time certain men of Chaldean descent came near and brought [malicious] accusations against the Jews. They said to King Nebuchadnezzar, O king, live forever!*
> *You, O king, have made a decree that every man who hears the sound of the horn, pipe, lyre, trigon, harp, dulcimer or bagpipe, and every kind of music shall fall down and worship the golden image,*
> *And that whoever does not fall down and worship shall be cast into the midst of a burning fiery furnace.*
> *There are certain Jews whom you have appointed and set over the affairs of the province of Babylon -- Shadrach, Meshach, and Abednego. These men, O king, pay no attention to you; they do not serve your gods or worship the golden image which you have set up." Daniel 3:8-12, AMP*

Nebuchadnezzar was so angry that he summoned Shadrach, Meshach, and Abednego to appear before him. He confronted them about their refusal to worship his gold statue and then gave them another chance to bow down in worship to his gold statue and save themselves from death. Nebuchadnezzar had never given anyone a second chance, but he did so for Shadrach, Meshach, and Abednego because of how valuable they were to him.

But in spite of that, these three young men refused to be intimidated by the king's threats. They looked him boldly in the eye and told him they will not bow down in worship of his gold statue – something no one had ever dared to do.

> *"Shadrach, Meshach, and Abednego answered the king, O Nebuchadnezzar, it is not necessary for us to answer you on this point. If our God Whom we serve is able to deliver us from the burning fiery furnace, He will deliver us out of your hand, O king. But if not, let it be known to you, O king, that we will not serve your gods or worship the golden image which you have set up!" Daniel 3:16-18, AMP*

The Bible says King Nebuchadnezzar was so furious with them that the anger distorted his face. He ordered that the furnace be heated up to become seven times hotter and then commanded his strongest soldiers to bind up Shadrach, Meshach, and Abednego and throw them into the blazing furnace. The flames were so hot that they instantly killed the strong soldiers who threw them into the furnace, but they themselves fell into the furnace without suffering any hurt.

> *"Then Nebuchadnezzar the king [saw and] was astounded, and he jumped up and said to his counselors, Did we not cast three men bound into the midst of the fire? They answered, True, O king. He answered, Behold, I see four men loose, walking in the midst of the fire, and they are not hurt! And the form of the fourth is like a son of the gods!"*
> *Daniel 3:24-25, AMP*

At the king's command, Shadrach, Meshach, and Abednego stepped out of the burning fiery furnace unhurt. The fire did not touch them, no single hair on their heads or bodies was singed, their clothing was not scorched, and they did not even smell of smoke.

When all the officials of Babylon saw and examined them, they were amazed. The king was overwhelmed by seeing such a miracle and had no choice but to praise and acknowledge the Most High.

> *"Then Nebuchadnezzar said, Blessed be the God of Shadrach, Meshach, and Abednego, Who has sent His*

angel and delivered His servants who believed in, trusted in, and relied on Him! And they set aside the king's command and yielded their bodies rather than serve or worship any god except their own God. Therefore I make a decree that any people, nation, and language that speaks anything amiss against the God of Shadrach, Meshach, and Abednego shall be cut in pieces and their houses be made a dunghill, for there is no other God who can deliver in this way! Then the king promoted Shadrach, Meshach, and Abednego in the province of Babylon." Daniel 3:28-30, AMP

Nebuchadnezzar who was worshipped as a god had no choice but to proclaim that only the Most High could accomplish such a great feat. If those three young men had compromised their faith in God to worship Nebuchadnezzar's statue, Nebuchadnezzar would never get to know about the Lord. But by their stance on the Word of God, those three young men declared the glory of God and made known His power to the heathen.

The Story Behind Their Story

"And the [Babylonian] king told Ashpenaz, the master of his eunuchs, to bring in some of the children of Israel, both of the royal family and of the nobility - Youths without blemish, well-favored in appearance and skillful in all wisdom, discernment, and understanding, apt in learning knowledge, competent

to stand and serve in the king's palace--and to teach them the literature and language of the Chaldeans. And the king assigned for them a daily portion of his own rich and dainty food and of the wine which he drank. They were to be so educated and so nourished for three years that at the end of that time they might stand before the king. Among these were of the children of Judah: Daniel, Hananiah, Mishael, and Azariah. The chief of the eunuchs gave them names: Daniel he called Belteshazzar [the king's attendant], Hananiah he called Shadrach, Mishael he called Meshach, and Azariah he called Abednego." Daniel 1:3-7, AMP

This scripture shows that Shadrach, Meshach, and Abednego were of royal blood, they were learned and highly intelligent, they were good looking and healthy. They were among the most outstanding young men from the tribe of Judah in terms of brilliance and radiance.

However, what the Babylonians failed to realize initially is that these three young men were also faithful to the Lord their God and to His Word. They were positively stubborn when it came to living for the Lord their God and obeying His Word.

First, these young men refused to be fed according to the king's diet, but according to their own diet. After ten days, they proved that their wisdom and knowledge about how to eat healthy and stay healthy was superior to that of the Babylonians (Daniel 1:11-15).

After their three years training, Nebuchadnezzar found them to be more intelligent and wiser than all the wise men and magicians in Babylon (Daniel 1:18-20).

In spite of all these achievements, these young men did not abandon their faith in God and they did not cease to practice His Word. But there are people today who feel they have no need for God because of their intellectual and academic achievements.

Just because they have become doctors or professors in one field or the other, they feel they have become too learned to study the Word of God and live according to its instructions. They feel they have become too big to submit to God and do as He commands. Instead of them to obey the Word of God, they question it and try to prove it wrong, just because they are celebrated intellectuals.

But ***no matter how learned a man may be, he can never be more learned than his Maker***. No matter what a man has invented and no matter his intellectual achievements, he can never be more intelligent than the One who created the heavens and the earth.

> *"Consider and understand, you stupid ones among the people! And you [self-confident] fools, when will you become wise? He Who planted the ear, shall He not hear? He Who formed the eye, shall He not see?" Psalm 94:8-9, AMP*

I also wish to add: He who formed the human brain, is He not intelligent?

Now, it's also interesting to note that Shadrach, Meshach, and Abednego were not willing to die because they were suffering hardship. They were not willing to die because they wanted to end their sorrows, for the Bible says they were living comfortably. Daniel 1:19 says "they became members of the king's court" (GNB) and Daniel 3:12 says they were "appointed and set over the affairs of the province of Babylon" (AMP).

These scriptures show that these young men were ready to die in defense of the truth of God's Word, in spite of the high positions of influence and power they occupied and in spite of the comfort, affluence, and privileges they were enjoying. They were prepared to let go all of these just to stand for the truth of God's Word.

However, there are many people today who would compromise their faith and twist the Word of God because they wouldn't want to offend their pay masters and lose their positions of power and influence. They claim to be children of God, yet they cannot stand in defense of the truth; they cannot fight for the truth. They would accept that the lie is the truth and that darkness is light, just to please people and keep their jobs or maintain their positions of power.

I thank God Shadrach, Meshach, and Abednego were not elderly men, but young people, so no one can say it was easy for them to be willing to die because they had already lived their lives to the full and enjoyed life.

These were young men who were just starting to live their lives and pursue their destinies, with many more years ahead of them. Yet they were ready to give up all those years, including everything they could achieve in the future ahead of them, just to defend the truth of God's Word.

It takes knowledge and deep conviction of God's Word for a youth to make such a decision. People who do not have the Word of God in them can never stand for God no matter the cost. However, God is seeking such people as Shadrach, Meshach, and Abednego that He may display His power and glory in them.

Until we experience the Word of God, we cannot see God's power and glory become manifest in our lives.

Chapter 5

THE SURE FOUNDATION

Unless we stand firm on the Word of God, His power and glory can never be manifested in us. Standing firm on the Word of God is the sure foundation for the Christian life. 2Chronicles 15: 2 says,

> *"The LORD is with you, while ye be with him; and if ye seek him, he will be found of you; but if ye forsake him, he will forsake you."*

God will only abide with us if we abide by His Word. If we depart from His Word, we part company with Him. If you want to see God do miraculous signs and wonders in and through your life, you have to stand firm on His Word. Only those who stand on the Word can stand up to the gods of this world. Only those who have been convicted and transformed by God's Word can stand up to the Nebuchadnezzars of this world.

If we abandon the Word of God and compromise with evil, the wicked will think that there is no God; they will think that those little idols they bow down to are the real God. But it takes a Shadrach, Meshach, and Abednego to reveal God to Nebuchadnezzar. If there is a man to stand firm on the Word of God, there is a God to prove His Word true.

It takes an unshakeable faith in the Word of God to produce such young men as Shadrach, Meshach, and Abednego. It takes conviction and love for the truth to stand for the truth.

Our world is in need of such men as Shadrach, Meshach, and Abednego – men of such character, knowledge, courage, and conviction who can dare the wicked in defense of the truth.

The reason we have many young people today who lack such conviction is because we have many leaders who lack conviction. The reason we have many young people who cannot stand up in defense of the truth is because we have many leaders who do not stand for the truth. The reason we have many young people who do not hesitate to compromise their faith is because we have many leaders who have long compromised their faith.

The reason we have many young people who have strayed from the faith is because we have many leaders who cannot show them the way. The reason we have many young people who do not imitate Christ in their lifestyle is because we have leaders who are not role models and cannot lead by example.

Therefore, the youths must stop following the examples of failed elders and leaders and begin to follow the examples of Christ. Hebrews 12:2 says we should be looking unto Jesus the author and finisher of our faith. So the youths must stop looking up to failed leaders who have disappointed the faith and look intently into the Word of Faith. James 1:25 says,

> *"But whoso looketh into the perfect law of liberty, and continueth therein, he being not a forgetful hearer, but a doer of the work, this man shall be blessed in his deed."*

When you look into the Word of God to live your life, you become liberated from the foolishness, faithlessness, corruption, and cowardice that has crippled many in the Church. When you live your life by the Word of God you become as bold as a lion; you become courageous enough to say no to evil and say yes to the truth, no matter what is at stake.

Chapter 6

THE FOUNDATION FOR LEADERSHIP SUCCESS

In 1Samuel 16, God rejected Saul from being king over His people. As people of God, we must learn to reject such people from being leaders over us. God's demand of righteous leadership does not only apply to the church; it also applies to governmental leadership and leadership in all spheres of life.

King Saul was a religious leader; he was a political leader, yet God rejected him, thereby giving us an example we should always follow. If God would not have certain kinds of people rule over us, then we too must not allow such people rule over us. If God has certain expectations from those who bear rule over His people, then we too must have expectations from those who bear rule over us.

The reason people become comfortable with unrighteous, corrupt, and incompetent leadership is because they themselves are unrighteous, corrupt, and incompetent. ***The leadership we tolerate is the leadership we deserve***. Subsequently, as God's people, we must learn to choose our leaders according to God's demands for leadership and reject people who have the same characteristics that were found in Saul from ruling over us.

On this note, it is important that we study the Scripture to know why God rejected Saul from being king over His people. This is because any leader who bears similar characteristics will never be acceptable to God. God will never accept or walk with any leader who is like Saul.

1. He Was Not Loyal To God, But Lived in Disobedience to God's Commands.

> *"And Samuel said to Saul, I will not return with you; for you have rejected the word of the Lord, and the Lord has rejected you from being king over Israel." 1Samuel 15:26, AMP*

Loyalty and obedience can never be separated. Loyalty begins with obedience. This is why ***a disobedient person can never be seen as a loyal person.*** God clearly stated to Samuel that one of the reasons He was rejecting Saul was because of his disobedience.

'Then the LORD said to Samuel, "I am sorry that I ever made Saul king, for he has not been loyal to me and has refused to obey my command."' 1Samuel 15:10-11, NLT

God's commands are God's instructions and His instructions are given to us through His Word, through His Spirit to us personally, or through his servants and prophets. This scripture shows that Saul was not subservient to God's Word. His life was not ruled by God's Word. He had no respect for God's Word and ordinances.

If a servant refuses to obey his master, he simply shows that he has no respect for his master. Similarly, people who have no respect for God's Word to obey it simply show that they have no respect for God.

Therefore, a person who has no respect for God is not qualified to bear rule over God's people. People who have no respect for God's Word to obey it, cannot and do not have the fear of God in them. The fear of the Lord is a product of knowing God, and knowing God comes from having knowledge of His Word.

God Values Obedience Over Material Things

When Saul disobeyed the Lord, Samuel said to him:

> *"What is more pleasing to the LORD: your burnt offerings and sacrifices or your obedience to his voice? Listen! Obedience is better than sacrifice, and submission is better than offering the fat of rams" 1Samuel 15:22, NLT*

There is nothing more pleasing to the Lord than a leader who lives and walks in obedience to God's principles and instruction. Saul thought that offering sacrifices and burnt offerings could make up for his disobedience and win him God's approval. But we have to learn from his experience that there is no amount of sacrifice we offer that can make up for a life of disobedience to God's instructions.

God is not a man to be appeased with goats, cows, sheep, and yams; He is not some deity that can be appeased with the blood of a fowl. It is either you do things His way or you go your way. You do not make a way for Him to follow, but He makes the way that you must follow. You do not set the standards for Him to accept, but you must live by His own standards.

Sacrifice can never be a substitute for a life of obedience. People who want to lead must learn to

follow God's leading. This is a principle that Saul failed to understand or live by, and after thousands of years some people are yet to understand this. Samuel said to Saul, God has rejected you because you have rejected God's command. People who reject (refuse to live in obedience to) God's command can never be suitable leaders.

2. He Dabbled Into The Occult.

Another reason God rejected Saul is because he got himself involved in the occult. Samuel said to him,

> *"Rebellion is as sinful as witchcraft. And stubbornness as bad as worshipping idols. So because you have rejected the command of the LORD, he has rejected you as king." 1Samuel 15:23b, NLT*

Samuel directly accused Saul of practicing witchcraft and he did not argue or deny it, which shows that he was culpable. In 1Samuel chapter 28, it is recorded that Saul consulted with a medium and practiced necromancy.

When people dabble into the occult they are in rebellion against God. ***No one can be a friend of the devil and be a lover of God.*** No one who receives counsel from the devil can do the will of God. No one who associates with the devil can lead people in the direction that God wants them to go. Those who partner with the devil do his bidding and wishes;

they can never pursue what is best for the people because the devil has no interest in the betterment of people's lives.

The Bible says the devil came to steal, kill, and destroy. If you look carefully you will observe that those who associate with the devil by dabbling into the occult do the same things. Therefore, when a person who is loyal to the devil comes into power, he will be there to execute the mandate of the kingdom of darkness.

When the Bible says the devil is the ruler of this world (John 12:31), we have to understand that he exercises this rulership by influencing the seats of power and leadership, which he accomplishes by putting his people there. The devil wants to fill leadership positions with people who are loyal to him so that he can control and influence the affairs and destinies of men. We cannot expect a servant of darkness to bring light to the people. We cannot expect a worker of iniquity to promote righteousness via his leadership position.

This is why as children of God, we must never support or promote godless people to rule over us. Leadership positions are positions of power and influence and whoever occupy these positions will influence people according to the power/spirit that influences them, either God or the devil.

It's a pity that some people think they need to dabble into the occult to get power with which to secure their positions. But the Bible says,

> *"It is an abomination [to God and men] for kings to commit wickedness, for a throne is established and made secure by righteousness (moral and spiritual rectitude in every area and relation)."*
> *Proverbs 16:12, AMP*

The devil has never done anything for the benefit of people, but for his own selfish interest; he has never been a blessing to anyone and will never be, because he does not have the capacity to bless. The devil has never used anyone for their own good because he does not care about what is good for you, but he only uses people to achieve his selfish aims and purposes.

Whatever the devil does for a person is an enticement to use him to destroy others before eventually destroying him. So, people who dabble into the occult do not only end up destroying themselves, they also makes themselves instruments in the hands of the devil to destroy others. This is why we must never support or promote such people to be rulers over us.

3. He Had More Fear And Respect For People Than For God. Another reason Saul was unfit to be a leader of God's people is because he had more fear for the people God gave him to lead than for the One who called him to lead the people. After Samuel rebuked him for his disobedience, he said to Samuel,

> *"I have sinned; for I have transgressed the commandment of the Lord and your words, because I feared the people and obeyed their voice."*
> *1Samuel 15:24*

This was his excuse for disobeying God's instruction. Saul was more interested in pleasing the people than in pleasing God; he cared more about people's opinion than God's opinion.

A person who lives to please people and is easily swayed by diverse human opinion is not fit to be a leader. A leader must know the truth of God's Word, must be ready to stand by the truth, and work to please God instead of people.

We cannot be men pleasers and be god-fearing leaders at the same time. People's opinion must never be a standard of right and wrong for a leader; the principles of God's Word should be his standard.

Human beings are wavering in their opinion and their opinions are often influenced by ignorance and selfish motives. But the Word of God abides forever; it is unwavering and unchanging from generation to generation.

Furthermore, a leader must be a person of conviction and not a double-minded person. James 1:8 says "A double minded man is unstable in all his ways." This means that a double-minded person does not have the stability required for leadership.

A leader must never be a person who is unsure of, or unable to determine, what is right or wrong, for leaders must have moral convictions and moral authority. A person who has no moral compass cannot lead people in the right direction. Leaders must know where they are going and how to get there, for if they cannot lead themselves in the right direction then they cannot lead people in the right direction.

Leadership is influence and a person whose life has not been influenced by God's Word is not qualified to lead God's people, either in the religious world or in government. Leadership is all about influencing people for good – for their own good and for the good of the society. Hence, leaders must know what is good and acceptable to God in order to be qualified to lead God's people.

Therefore, a person who has more respect for people's opinion than for God's Word will be a leadership failure. A person who has fear for people (especially a set of people or cabal) more than for God, can never end up doing what is good for the people; for whatever is not good and acceptable in the eyes of God can never be good for the people.

The Necessity for Spiritual Maturity

"For we wrestle not against flesh and blood, but against principalities, against powers, against the rulers of the darkness of this world, against spiritual wickedness in high places." Ephesians 6:12

This scripture shows that the leaders of spiritual wickedness always seek access to high places from where they can influence things for the kingdom of darkness, for they know these high positions are positions of power and influence.

Spiritual maturity is crucial to leadership because the rulers of darkness always target the seats of power and rulership on earth so they can usurp the powers of those offices to advance their wicked agenda.

Therefore, people who occupy these seats of human leadership find themselves in contention with the powers of darkness. This is why a leader must be spiritually sound, with the spiritual capacity to withstand and resist these satanic powers and ensure that the will of God comes to bear in his leadership and in the affairs of the people.

But a leader who is empty of God's Word and Spirit and is spiritually dormant is ignorant of spiritual matters, and such people are not fit for leadership in a world as ours with so much satanic influence and manipulation. 1Timothy 3:5 says, "For if a man does not know how to rule his own household, how is he to take care of the church of God?"

This scripture is not only applicable to religious leaders, but also applicable to political leaders and leaders in the corporate world. One of the reasons people abuse their positions of leadership is because of immaturity. ***A person who is not fit to lead himself aright is not fit to lead other people.***

Leadership does not only demand intellectual maturity, it also demands character and spiritual maturity; for we cannot afford to have unstable people leading us – people who lack conviction about right and wrong but are easily tossed to and fro by every wind of knowledge and doctrine. Ephesians 4:14 says,

> *"That we henceforth be no more children, tossed to and fro, and carried about with every wind of doctrine, by the sleight of men, and cunning craftiness, whereby they lie in wait to deceive"*

This scripture says such people are like children, which means they are immature; are easily carried away, which means they lack conviction; and they are easily deceived or misled, which means they lack wisdom and prudence.

If Saul had the necessary maturity, he would not have more fear and respect for the people than for God; he would not have easily cowered under pressure.

4. He Lacked Reverence For The Things Of God. 1Samuel 13:9 says,

> *"So Saul said, Bring me the burnt offering and the peace offerings. And he offered the burnt offering [which he was forbidden to do]."(AMP)*

To have reverence for the things of God includes having respect for God's servants, and for His ordinances. God is a God of precepts and order; He has set forth things in His Kingdom in an organized manner, and He expects us to abide by them. A leader who has little or no regard for the things God has ordained simply shows that he has little or no regard for God.

Saul was chosen and anointed king, yet he decided to usurp the functions and office of Prophet Samuel. A leader must understand what God has called him to do and stay within the confines of his assignment. A leader must also acknowledge what God has called other people to do and have regard for them.

Just because he was the king, Saul thought he could do what he liked and function wherever he pleased; he thought he could show lack of respect for the person and office of Prophet Samuel without consequences.

A person who cannot carry out the functions of his office while also allowing others to carry out the responsibilities of their office, is not fit to be a leader. A true leader must have regard for God, the things of God, the house of God, and the servants of God.

You cannot disregard and disrespect God's anointed and not show disregard and disrespect for God.

Just like Saul, some people think they can belittle the office and calling of God's servants, usurp their authority and treat them with disrespect, just because they have come to occupy some high position in government. Your position in government does not exempt you from showing regard for God, for His ordinances, and for the people He has ordained.

Your governmental position does not belittle the importance of God's servants. Just as Saul was not superior to the person who anointed him into the office of a king, your position in government does not make God's anointed servants inferior to you. ***The head that receives the oil can never be superior to the hand that pours the oil.***

Also, having more money than a servant of God does not make his ministry irrelevant, because there are things that money cannot buy.

God rejected Saul as king because he showed disregard for the things of God and for the office and person of his servant, Samuel. People who do the same thing today stand to be rejected just like Saul was, for God is the same yesterday, today, and forever (Hebrews 13:8). People cannot reject the things that God has ordained and then expect God to find them acceptable.

The Necessity for Superior Knowledge

"The fear of the Lord is the foundation of true knowledge, but fools despise wisdom and discipline." Proverbs 1:7, NLT

Knowledge of God's Word is superior to every other knowledge, for it is the Word that brought the world into existence. One of the reasons people despise God's Word is because it disciplines and chastises us. Transformation often takes place through discipline. When people despise and reject God's Word, they despise and reject the knowledge, wisdom, and discipline that would make them succeed in life.

A person who has little or no knowledge of God's Word, who has no respect for it to live by it, is not qualified to be a leader over God's people. This is because such a person will neither lead with the fear of God nor with God's influence. Saul was not rejected because he did not know politics, because he was uneducated, or because he lacked leadership skills, but because the Word of God and the fear of God were not in him.

The qualification for leadership is more than being educated, having charisma, and having the ability to mobilize or inspire people; one must have the quality, character, discipline, maturity, and ability to inspire people for the right things and for the right reasons. No matter how educated, intelligent, or talented a person may be, he is not fit for leadership if he does not have the Word of God and the fear of God in him.

If Saul had superior knowledge he wouldn't have showed such disregard and lack of reverence for the things of God.

5. He Lacked Wisdom And Common Sense.

Another factor that destroyed the reign of King Saul was his lack of wisdom and common sense. His reign was marked by unbelievable displays of foolishness.

In 1Samuel 14:24-32, King Saul forced his soldiers who were in the midst of battle to swear an oath that they would abstain from eating (fast) throughout that day, with the condition that anyone who violated the oath will be under a curse.

Such an oath and the curse attached to it was uncalled for, was not by divine direction, and made no sense because soldiers need strength for battle, and that strength comes from food. Any military general or strategist will tell you that an army starved of provision is an army waiting to be defeated. Wars are not won on empty stomach, which is why in times of war one army often tries to destroy or cut off their enemies from food supply.

Due to Saul's rash and foolish decision, the army of the Israelites could not fight that day to their full strength and capacity, and they could not secure the kind of victory they were capable of.

> *"Then Jonathan said, My father has troubled the land. See how my eyes have brightened because I tasted a little of this honey. How much better if the men had eaten freely today of the spoil of their enemies which they found! For now the slaughter of the Philistines has not been great. They smote the Philistines that day from Michmash to Aijalon. And the people were very faint." 1Samuel 14:29-31, AMP*

Towards the end of the day, the soldiers of Israel were so exhausted and famished because they had fought all day without tasting any food, and this led them into sinning against the Lord their God. The Bible says,

> *"They chased and killed the Philistines all day from Micmash to Aijalon, growing more and more faint. That evening they rushed for the battle plunder and*

> *butchered the sheep, goats, cattle, and calves, but they ate them without draining the blood."*
> *1 Samuel 14:31-33, NLT*

Thus, by his lack of wisdom, Saul led the people into sinning against the Lord. One of the consequences of foolish leadership is that a foolish leader will always lead the people into disaster. ***Foolishness and leadership should never be in partnership. A person who lacks wisdom and common sense has no business with leadership.*** The Bible says wisdom is the principal or most important thing (Proverbs 4:7), and this is especially true for leadership. We must never consent to having foolish people rule over us, for ***foolish leadership endangers the lives and destiny of a people.***

People who refuse to embrace wisdom must never be promoted or support for leadership positions. When people promote a fool to rule over them, it simply shows that they are more foolish than the person. Psalm 119:130 says,

> *"The entrance of Your words gives light; It gives understanding to the simple."(NKJV)*

This shows that people lack wisdom because they do not study and give heed to the Word of God. Foolishness is a sign that a person does not know and live by the Word of God, and such a person is not fit to bear rule over God's people. A person who is full of the Word cannot be filled with the spirit of foolishness Proverbs 1:1-4 says,

> *"These are the proverbs of Solomon, David's son, king of Israel. Their purpose is to teach people wisdom and discipline, to help them understand the insights of the wise. Their purpose is to teach people to live disciplined and successful lives, to help them do what is right, just, and fair. These proverbs will give insight to the simple, knowledge and discernment to the young." Proverbs 1:1-4, NLT*

This shows that wisdom is instrumental to success in every area of life and that everyone can acquire wisdom; it shows that wisdom is available and within the reach of everyone. Therefore, people who lack wisdom show that they lack the discipline to be saddled with leadership responsibilities. A person who does not have the discipline to sit down and study God's Word to improve on himself does not have what it takes to bring meaningful improvement to the lives of the people.

The Necessity of Wisdom

> *"The fear of the LORD is the foundation of wisdom. Knowledge of the Holy One results in good judgment." Proverbs 9:10, NLT*

Wisdom is one of the top qualities of leadership and it is a product or result of the fear of the Lord, which of course comes from knowing and doing God's Word. The fear of the Lord that produces wisdom does not only come from knowledge of the Word but by also doing the Word. ***People who know the Word but do not practice it can never be examples of wisdom.*** This shows that the Word of God is the foundation of true leadership; it is the foundation for leadership success.

This is because in the Word are principles that make for leadership success. People who do not know and practice these principles are bound to experience mediocrity and failure in leadership in all areas of life; either as a family leader (head of your family), political leader, or religious leader. The principles of leadership enshrined in God's Word have no bounds or limitation; they are relevant to all aspects and levels of leadership.

2Timothy 2:15 also says we should study to make ourselves approved of God so that we can rightly handle the Word of God and apply it. Also, this scripture are not only applicable to religious leaders, but also applicable to political leaders and leaders in the corporate world. They show that leadership is not for spiritual babes.

A person who cannot study to develop himself intellectually, morally, emotionally, and spiritually is not fit for leadership. This is because man does not only have a body; he is also made up of a spirit and a soul, and all these aspects of man need to be developed in order to achieve good success.

People who lack wisdom can never have God's approval. If God cannot approve of such people to lead His people, then we must never approve of such people to lead us or follow their example, for ***people who follow in the footsteps of foolishness never end well.***

One of the reasons we have experienced tragic leadership in our nation is because we ignore these principles and choose to walk by sentiments. We choose our leaders on the basis of sentiments and not on the basis of principles, yet we keep wondering why things have not changed for the better.

Leadership is crucial to the development of a people or nation, and until we the people change our attitude we will continue to experience failed leadership. We cannot keep producing leaders who are not acceptable to God and expect things to turn out better in our nation. We cannot have a godly nation without godly leaders.

If we want to see the goodness of God become manifest in our nation, we must set aside sentiments and begin to choose for ourselves leaders after God's heart. ***When a nation has right leaders, things begin to go right; when a nation has good leaders, good things begin to happen to its people***. When a nation has leaders whose lives are influenced by God's Word, the blessings of His Word begin to manifest in that nation. This shows that the Word of God is crucial to leadership success and national progress.

People always lead by example; its either they're leading by good example or they're leading by bad example. If God was sorry that He made Saul King over Israel, we will always end up being sorry for choosing people like him to rule over us.

Chapter 7

THE MANUAL FOR MARITAL SUCCESS

The necessity for success in marriage can never be over-emphasized because marriage stands to affect most of our lives. The legacy we leave for our future generation is often determined by the kind of marriage we have. The Bible says,

> *"Enjoy life with your beloved wife during all the days of your fleeting life that God has given you on earth during all your fleeting days; for that is your reward in life and in your burdensome work on earth." Ecclesiastes 9:9, NET*

This scripture clearly shows that God wants us to have a happy and fulfilling marriage experience here on earth. He did not only tell us so, but He has also shown us how to do so in His Word. This is because success in marriage is crucial to our wellbeing.

Our relationship with our spouse can affect our relationship with our children, our children's relationship with their own spouse, and our children's relationship with their own children. This goes to show how crucial marriage is in shaping our lives and the lives of the future generation.

At this juncture, let me begin to correct some wrong impression about marriage. Marriage is a covenant relationship between a man and a woman, and not between a man and a man, a woman and a woman, or a boy and a girl. We relate with people on a daily basis and at different levels. But marriage is the deepest and most intimate level of relationship between a man and a woman. Jesus said,

> *"Have you never read that He Who made them from the beginning made them male and female, and said, For this reason a man shall leave his father and mother and shall be united firmly (joined inseparably) to his wife, and the two shall become one flesh?"*
> *Matthew 19:4-5, AMP*

Marriage was instituted by God, and for us to succeed in it we need to learn from the One who instituted it. Now let us look at this illustration. If your Mercedes Benz car should have a problem, you do not take it to a Toyota repairer shop for repairs, but you take it to a Mercedes Benz repair shop. Also, you don't study the manual of a Samsung TV to learn how to operate a Sony TV.

So why is it that when it comes to marriage we do not apply the same common sense? A Biology student who spends time studying Accounting textbooks can never excel in Biology because he has been studying the wrong textbooks.

Marriage was invented and instituted by God, and if we want to succeed in it or fix it, we should humbly go to Him. The Bible is God's manual for the Man He created. God's manual for Man's success contains information on how the male and female he created can succeed in their relationship.

It is also important to mention that marriage is not a contract because in a contract each partner looks out for his/her own benefit and is solely interested in what he/she can get out of it. But marriage is a covenant because in a covenant, each partner looks out for the benefit and wellbeing of the other; they look out for what is mutually beneficial. This is why ***people who approach their marriage with a contract mentality find it difficult or impossible to succeed in it.***

Therefore, here are some important insights from God's Word that can help us have a happy and successful marriage.

1. Marriage Demands Maturity

In Matthew 19:5 Jesus said,

> *"And God said, 'For this reason a man will leave his father and mother and unite with his wife, and the two will become one.'" GNB*

This clearly shows that marriage is not for underage persons. ***Marriage is not for boys and girls but for men and women.*** The Greek word translated 'wife' in this scripture means a woman. A boy cannot be a husband and a girl cannot be a wife. It takes a man to be a husband and it takes a woman to be a wife. God did not say a boy shall leave his father's house and be joined to a girl.

Another angle to this is that childhood is synonymous with immaturity and adulthood is synonymous with maturity. This shows that marriage demands maturity – in body, soul (mind, emotion), and spirit. Marriage demands maturity in the way we think, talk, reason, and act. ***Marriage is not an institution for adults who are yet to outgrow their childish ways of thinking, talking, and behaving.***

Many marriages have been destroyed by lack of maturity. But ***knowledge of God's Word builds maturity into people.*** A person who has not been transformed by God's Word is not prepared for succeeding in the marriage institution. (Please take note that I did not say a person who does not go to church, but a person whose life has not been transformed by God's Word.)

Such a person may be biologically (physically) ready, but not emotionally and spiritually ready for marital success. Marriage is not as simple as ABC; ***it takes physical, emotional, and spiritual commitment and maturity to succeed in marriage***. Marriage demands maturity in the way you talk. Apostle Paul said,

> *"When I was a child, I talked like a child, I thought like a child, I reasoned like a child; now that I have become a man, I am done with childish ways and have put them aside." 1Corinthians 13:11, AMP*

You cannot talk childishly and carelessly and expect to have a happy marriage. We build our marriage relationship with our words and actions, and so we must watch the way we talk and our use of words.

We have to understand that our words leave a more lasting impact and impression on people. This is because while a cane hurts the body, words hurt the soul; and a hurt in the soul lasts longer than the pain on the body.

The way you talk to your spouse will determine the way you relate. You cannot speak to your spouse like a child and expect your spouse to treat you like an adult. Therefore, you must learn to talk to your spouse the way you want your spouse to talk to you.

2. Marriage Demands Discipline & Self-control. Proverbs 5:23 says,

> *"They die because they have no self-control. Their utter stupidity will send them to their graves." (GNB)*

Lack of discipline and self-control has destroyed many promising relationships and has buried many marriages. ***Lack of self-control is an ingredient for marital failure.*** One of the attributes of a child is that a child always wants everything that looks attractive to him, and it's a pity that many married people still have this childish trait in them. In spite of the person they already have in their lives, they still want to have some other persons that look attractive to them.

An adult who wants to have every attractive person that he/she sees, is on the same level with a child who wants to have every attractive toy that he sees in the supermarket.

3. Marriage Demands Communication

> *"Be happy with your own wife. Enjoy the woman you married while you were young." Proverbs 5:18, ERV*

This means that as a married person you must be ready to talk to and listen to your spouse. One of the problems some men have is that they mostly talk to their spouse but hardly listen to them. Your wife does not only have ears; she also has a mouth. Your wife does not only have a pretty face; she also has a brain that is more sophisticated than any computer in the world.

Many marriages lack happiness because of absence of proper communication. One of the ways to enjoy your marriage is by communicating with our spouse.

4. Marriage Demands Team Work

> *"Two people are better off than one, for they can help each other succeed. If one person falls, the other can reach out and help. But someone who falls alone is in real trouble" Ecclesiastes 4:9-10, NLT*

Successful couples are those who make good use of all the resources that God has given to both of them. This scripture quote has shown that ***one of the purposes of marriage is for two people to help each other succeed, and not to compete with each other.*** When a married person is only interested in his or her own success, the marriage will face challenges because everyone has a desire to be successful.

Therefore, marriage demands selflessness and not selfishness. You can afford to be selfish when you are alone, but when you become a couple you cannot afford to be selfish, because ***selfishness defeats the very purpose of your being a couple.***

5. Marriage Demands Transparency

> *'So you must stop telling lies. "You must always speak the truth to each other," because we all belong to each other in the same body."' Ephesians 4:25, ERV*

Marriage does not demand secrecy. Countries and governments may thrive by keeping secrets in their relationship with other countries and governments, but marriage does not. Secrets destroy marriages because they inspire distrust.

The moment trust flies out of a marriage, the marriage begins to stand on one leg, which means it may not stand well for long. ***A marriage that lacks trust can never be happy and wholesome.*** That is why people who are not prepared and willing to be truthful, honest, and transparent from the start are not ready to succeed in marriage.

6. Marriage Demands Understanding

1Peter 3:7 says, "you husbands must live with your wives with the proper understanding that they are more delicate than you" (GNB). This scripture shows that God wants a man to live with his wife with understanding. Proverbs 19:14 says, *"only the LORD can give an understanding wife" (NLT).* This scripture also shows that God wants a woman to live with her husband with understanding.

To lack understanding means to be unreasonable. In marriage we must learn to be reasonable and try to understand our spouse's opinion and point of view; we must always try to put ourselves in their shoes and learn to look at things from their own perspective.

7. Marriage Demands A Forgiving Spirit

> *"Love prospers when a fault is forgiven, but dwelling on it separates close friends." Proverbs 17:9, NLT*

This scripture shows that an unforgiving spirit destroys love and friendship. One of the reasons some people's love for their spouse has gone cold is because they have an unforgiving spirit and they keep record of their spouse's wrongs. But 1Corinthians 13:5 says love "keeps no record of being wronged" (NLT).

Some people wrongly think that holding grievances against their spouse will make their spouse to change for the better. But it does not; it destroys love and affection.

Your spouse is the closest person to you, which means she will have more opportunities to offend you than any other person. Therefore, you must understand this and have a heart that is open to forgive.

Design Your Own Marital Success

These Bible principles are the key to enjoying peace, affection, and happiness in your marriage. Galatians 6:16 says,

> *"Peace and mercy be upon all who walk by this rule [who discipline themselves and regulate their lives by this principle], even upon the [true] Israel of God!" (AMP)*

If you're not ready to study God's Word and practice it, then you're not ready to enjoy your marriage. Marital success does not happen by luck or chance; it happens by design. Therefore, begin to design your own marital success.

CONCLUSION

THE GUARANTEE OF SUCCESS

The Word of God is crucial for succeeding in every area of life. When we search the Word, we are seeking the secrets of success. When we study the Word we are acquiring the understanding and strength required for success. However, James 1:22-24 says,

> *"Do what God's teaching says; don't just listen and do nothing. When you only sit and listen, you are fooling yourselves. Hearing God's teaching and doing nothing is like looking at your face in the mirror and doing nothing about what you saw. You go away and immediately forget how bad you looked." (ERV)*

Success by the Word comes from not only knowing the Word, but also practicing it. ***Knowing the principles of success in God's Word does not guarantee success, but doing them surely does.*** People who practice the Word of God can never be the same or remain at the same level.

The difference between successful believers and unsuccessful believers is that while the later only receive the Word, the former do something with the Word they receive. ***When we live by the Word, we are putting into practice the principles for success.***

Therefore, I strongly urge you to do something with the knowledge and insights you have received from this book, for that is the key to succeeding in every area of your life.

You are blessed!

REFERENCES

Scriptures marked as (NLT) are taken from the *Holy Bible,* New Living Translation, copyright © 1996, 2004, 2007 by Tyndale House Foundation. Used by permission of Tyndale House Publishers, Inc., Carol Stream, Illinois 60188. All rights reserved.

Scripture quotations marked (NKJV) are taken from the Holy Bible, New King James Version, copyright © 1982 by Thomas Nelson, Inc.

Scripture quotations marked (AMP) are taken from THE AMPLIFIED BIBLE, Old Testament copyrights © 1965, 1987 by Zondervan Corporation. The Amplified New Testament copyright © 1958, 1987 by the Lockman Foundation. Used by permission.

Scriptures marked as (GNB) are taken from the Good News Bible Second Edition © 1992 by American Bible Society. Used by permission.

Scripture quotations marked (ERV) are taken from the HOLY BIBLE: EASY-TO-READ VERSION © 2008 by World Bible Translation Center, Inc. and used by permission.

Scripture Quotations marked (NET) are taken from The NET Bible® Copyright © 1996-2006 by Biblical Studies Press (BSP) Used by permission, All rights reserved.

ABOUT THE AUTHOR

Apostle Francis Anso was born into a Catholic family at Amamong Okobo, Okobo Local Government Area, Akwa Ibom Ṣtate, Nigeria. He later changed to Mount Zion Light House Full Gospel Church.

He worked for several years and trained as a Deacon at Mount Zion Light House Full Gospel Church, Itiam Assembly.

He later received God's call to shepherd His people as the General Overseer of The Land of Truth Fellowship, a.k.a "Isong Akpaniko".

He has been happily married to Evangelist (Mrs.) Mercy Francis Effiong for over thirty years and they have been blessed with four children.

He is a servant of God whom God uses to deliver people from demonic oppression and possession, heal the sick, restore barren wombs, heal broken relationships and restore broken homes. He is a man of fervent prayer and is passionately committed to seeing people become prosperous and successful.

This book will help you deepen your experience with God, discover your spiritual potentials, and live in dominion over the power of the enemy.

www.ingramcontent.com/pod-product-compliance
Lightning Source LLC
La Vergne TN
LVHW040948150826
845672LV00002B/589

* 9 7 9 8 8 4 8 4 7 3 0 5 6 *